Anonymus

The Blind Boy of the Island

Anonymus

**The Blind Boy of the Island**

ISBN/EAN: 9783742834010

Manufactured in Europe, USA, Canada, Australia, Japa

Cover: Foto ©Andreas Hilbeck / pixelio.de

Manufactured and distributed by brebook publishing software (www.brebook.com)

Anonymus

**The Blind Boy of the Island**

THE LIFELESS BODY WAS WASHED UP BY THE TIDE.
[*Page* 128

# THE BLIND BOY OF THE ISLAND.

BY THE AUTHOR OF "URSULA'S PROMISE."

LONDON:
THE RELIGIOUS TRACT SOCIETY;
56, PATERNOSTER ROW; 65, ST. PAUL'S CHURCHYARD;
AND 164, PICCADILLY.

# THE BLIND BOY OF THE ISLAND

## CHAPTER I.

THE wind blew furiously over the little island of Jersey; the waves, so blue, so tranquil but a few hours before, dashed angrily upon the rocky coast, and now and again a flash of lightning gleamed through the heavy clouds, and the thunder rolled ominously over the roofs of the cottages on the sea-shore.

As one dazzling flash followed another Antoinette Le Breton crossed herself and muttered an Ave Maria, for she was a devout Catholic; but the cottage seemed lonely in the stormy evening, as she listened eagerly for the step of her husband, who should be returning home from his day's work in the town. Presently he came; even through the noise of wind and rain Antoinette could hear the welcome step, firm, strong, and blithe as ever; and he was singing too, perhaps to cheer his heart and beguile the way:

> "Mary, Mother, shield us through life;
> Protect us from the ocean's strife;
> Calm the wild sea, bid tempests cease;
> Through thee we reach the shore in peace."

The young wife smiled as she caught the familiar words. "He has a brave heart, has Stephen," she said to herself. "There is not many a man could sing through such a storm, but then he has a good conscience, and his hymn is a prayer."

An honest, frank face was that of Stephen Le Breton as it appeared at the kitchen door. "Oh, Stephen, I'm glad you're safe!" cried Antoinette, clinging to him as to one who had braved a great danger, while tears, hitherto repressed, gushed up into her eyes.

The great strong man smiled down upon her little figure, and a big but not ungentle hand rested on the head she had buried in his arm.

"Why, what a foolish child it is!" he said; "was not Mary, the Mother of Mercy, watching over me in the storm? Could she not protect me, 'Toinette?"

"Ah, yes, yes, Stephen; and yet it might be"—and then Antoinette hesitated, and her voice sunk to a whisper—"and yet, Stephen, there are those who pray to her, but still fall into terrible danger."

Stephen looked grave, and whistled softly—a sure sign that something perplexed him; but presently he brightened up, and raising his young wife's bowed head with both his big brown hands, said, "Get the supper now, little one, for I am both cold and hungry; and trust your old Stephen to the Blessed Mother who has brought him safely through many a storm on land and sea."

The thought of Stephen cold and hungry was sufficient to rouse all Antoinette's housewifely instincts; and soon a good supper was set out, to which husband and wife applied themselves with hearty appetite, and scarcely even noticed, as they talked, that the storm was abating.

"I met the good Père Guillaume in town to-day," said Stephen at length. "There has been bad news; the English boat has gone down in the storm, only just outside our own harbour, and every soul on board lost."

"May God have mercy on them!" ejaculated Antoinette, crossing herself piously as she spoke; "I had not heard of it, Stephen."

"Nay, it takes long for news to find its way here, though 'tis but a mile and a half from the town," said Stephen. "Still I thought may be that some one coming this road might have told it, for it's on every one's lips, and the old saying is, 'Ill news travels apace.'"

"And what else did the Père Guillaume say, Stephen?" questioned Antoinette. "Did he tell you aught of that relic of the blessed Margaret Mary he has promised me?"

Le Breton shook his head. "He said naught to me of relics; he did not even ask if you were well, 'Toinette. His mind was full of the thought of these poor souls called into eternity, and he bid me pray for them; and you too should say a rosary on their behalf, he said; and the Holy Mass to-morrow will be offered up for them."

Antoinette was evidently considering something; "To-morrow is Saturday," she said. "I was going into the market with some eggs, and Mrs. Le Fevre asked me to take her butter. I might start early, Stephen, and so be at the Mass, for the good father says it at six o'clock. Poor souls! They need all the prayers they can get, even such as mine."

"Ay, do so, little wife," responded Stephen. "And I will rise too, and go with you; we can eat a bit on the way, and let breakfast go for once—it will be a little penance to offer to the Blessed Virgin for these poor souls, and maybe avail to spare them one pain in purgatory."

Antoinette rose now and began clearing the table. If she was to start thus early in the morning, some little household duties must be attended to over-night, and as Mrs. Le Breton was a thrifty housewife she found plenty of work for her head and hands as she tripped about the cottage with nimble footsteps, singing the refrain of the hymn which was a favourite with both her and Stephen:

"Calm the wild sea, bid tempests cease;
Through thee we reach the shore in peace."

Dark as it was now, the heavy clouds had rolled away, the waves were lulling, and the wind had almost died to a whispering breeze. Stephen Le Breton stood in his cottage doorway looking out seaward with calm, placid face, listening to his wife's sweet voice, and now and then joining in with a note or two. He was very happy with that bright blithe Antoinette of his; it had been a good day for him when he had won such a prize from her home just over in Normandy; he could not have found such a thrifty housewife in Jersey, nor, above all, such a devout Catholic; and the Le Bretons had always been Catholics from the old long-gone-by days, when the little island had been a possession of the French, and had held the same religious creed.

Few of such were there in Jersey; and Le Breton was proud of his name and his Catholic faith; and thus he had, by the counsel of the priest, Père Guillaume, sought a wife from the simple and devout Norman peasantry, who rested happily in the possession of the religion of their forefathers, nor knew those doubts and longings and desires which the père declared came from the enemy of souls.

One shadow rested on the happy household; but it was not a heavy one, for had not the priest declared that by a course of prayers offered to the Virgin Mother, by invocation of the saints, and by a special devotion to one—the blessed Margaret Mary Alacoque—Stephen and Antoinette Le Breton would yet rejoice over a living child? They were hearing much of the blessed Margaret Mary just then; true, Stephen had said that he liked better the saints of olden days, than those new devotions, and that he would rather call the holy apostles to their aid—his own patron St. Stephen, for example.

But the Père Guillaume had been displeased at this, and Le Breton had done penance for such presumptuous words; and now that the feast of the blessed Margaret approached, he had bidden Antoinette make a novena or nine days' prayer to her, that she might obtain for her the blessing of a child to live and comfort her—a daughter who should be called Margaret Mary. And he had promised, too, a relic of the holy woman who had been, it was said, privileged to look so often upon the form of Christ in glorious vision, and hear Him say, "Learn of Me; for I am meek and lowly in heart."

Day by day, Antoinette Le Breton longed and waited for that precious relic; and, as she waited, she thought much of her whose aid she was about to invoke, and arranged in her own mind the number and kind of prayers she would say during the special nine days so soon approaching.

The morning after the storm was calm and fair; the blue waves looked as if they could never foam and rage so angrily against the rocks, yet some huge heaps of sea-weed lay upon the shore as a silent proof of their rough work.

Antoinette and her husband rose early, and made their way to the town. It was a long walk, and the heavy market-basket must be carried, in which Mrs. Le Fevre's golden butter and the large snowy eggs from Mrs. Le Breton's hens had been safely packed before the day had fairly dawned.

But neither Stephen nor his bright little Norman wife minded the long walk or the heavy basket, for were they not going to pray for God's mercy on the souls of those for whom Holy Mass would be offered that morning? poor souls which had, may be, to suffer countless years in the fires of purgatory until released by the prayers and penances of those who remembered them on earth! Ah! we who smile at the superstitious faith, at the ignorant credulity which receives such teaching, let us look into our hearts, and see if with higher, purer instruction and belief we have the earnest, self-denying piety of those we pity, nay, perhaps, almost despise.

So Stephen and Antoinette walked on until the church was reached, and the huge market-basket carefully deposited in the porch, where no one would ever think of meddling with it. That done, they passed into the dim building, already filled with worshippers, and said many a Pater and Ave as the Mass went on.

Coming out one of the last of the congregation, Antoinette saw Père Guillaume in the doorway, and understood from a sign that she was to wait behind to speak to him.

"I have here for you the relic, dear child," said the priest, in his broken English, as he took a small glass case from a breast-pocket.

Antoinette kissed it reverently as the père held it towards her, then placed it carefully in her bosom.

"And the novena begins, you understand, to-morrow; and upon the ninth day you will come here to receive the most holy sacraments, my child," explained the priest.

"Ah! oui, mon père, je comprends—I understand," said Antoinette, smiling and blushing with delight at her possession. "Have I not made many a novena in my own country? one to St. Anne, too, which did not indeed get me the blessing. I desired; but doubtless the dear saint knew it was not for my good."

"Ah! c'est vrai, ma fille," responded the priest. "Do not the Holy Scriptures teach us that sometimes we ask and have not because we ask amiss? But patience, courage, mon enfant, the blessed Marguerite will grant this request;" and raising his hand in benediction, Père Guillaume re-entered the church, and Antoinette went her way.

Those who knew the pretty Norman peasant thought she had never looked more bright and smart than at that Saturday market. She had a smile and a merry word for all, and seemed, indeed, so joyful of heart that old Martha Vallère, at the next stall, said,

"What ails thee, child? thou seemest to have some secret on thy mind which thou canst scarce keep?"

"Ah! and you have guessed well, mother!" cried 'Toinette, clapping her hands like a gleeful child. "I have a secret; but I will tell you, or you shall guess. What think you I carry here, close to my heart, Mother Vallère?"

"A picture of that well-favoured husband of thine, doubtless," said the old woman, smiling, too, in her grim way. "'Tis not hard to guess thy secret, Antoinette Le Breton."

"Nay, better than that, mother," replied the cheery little wife; "Stephen's picture is safe at home on the wall of our best parlour, and like him it is, too. Guess again, Mother Vallère."

And the old peasant guessed, but never right; and so at last Antoinette told of the precious relic which the good Père Guillaume had entrusted to her keeping.

"You foolish child!" said old Martha, when she had heard the tale. "Do you think a morsel of linen worn by any one, even if they're good and holy, could do you any good? I don't know anything of your Margaret Mary; there's not a word of her in my Bible; but I'll tell you what there is in it. There's the story of a woman who had no child, and she went every day to the temple and prayed to God—*to God*, do you hear, Antoinette?—and not to one of His creatures; and her prayer was heard, and after a while a child was born to her, and she called his name Samuel."

Antoinette had some indistinct idea that such talk was sinful, that Père Guillaume would not approve of it, and if she listened she must confess such listening to be a sin. She did not want to do this, for might not "the father" forbid friendship with her Protestant neighbours, and was she not going to the sacraments of confession and communion upon the ninth day of her special prayer?

So Antoinette put the tips of her taper fingers in her ears and shook her head. "Peace, peace, old Martha," she said, gently. "Do you forget that as a good Catholic it would be sin in me to listen to such talk. I know nothing of your Bible—the saints forbid! But the good Père Guillaume has told me the story of blessed Margaret Mary, the dear and holy nun to whom our Divine Lord gloriously revealed Himself, and, pointing to His sacred heart, bade her tell abroad how that heart beats with love for men. To her I will address myself, and she will present my prayer to Jesus, and gain me the favour I seek."

So Mrs. Le Breton returned to the thought of her butter and eggs, whispering a passing Ave as she pressed the relic closer to her heart, while old Martha muttered crossly, "Blessed Margaret! Sacred heart! The poor thing's head is quite turned; and yet there's the teaching of the Bible as clear as day, and it says, 'Whatsoever ye shall ask the Father in My name'—the name of Jesus—'believing, ye shall receive.'"

## CHAPTER II.

THE nine days' prayer to the departed nun was over; earnestly and devoutly had poor little Antoinette gone through the prescribed routine, offering all for the blessing she so much desired, and which she firmly believed would be granted her by the blessed Margaret Mary's intercession. But days passed into weeks, weeks rolled into months, and a year and more went by, yet the Le Bretons had a childless home. Clearly the saints had forgotten them.

The little wife seemed less blithe than formerly, for indeed it was a deep and bitter disappointment.

Let Père Guillaume talk of being resigned; let him tell her that she must persevere in prayers, in fasting and mortification, and in the hearing of Mass, if she would propitiate the blessed in heaven. Antoinette stoutly refuses to make another novena, for does not old Martha Vallère wag her head sagely every time they meet, and say, "So that good woman couldn't help you after all, child? You'd better be like her I told you of out of my old Bible."

However, when Stephen was a little more grave and sad, Antoinette a shade less bright and gleeful; when the poor woman had given up praying to the saints about the matter, a little son was given to Mrs. Le Breton; not the desired daughter, and therefore we may conclude that blessed Margaret Mary had nothing to do with it.

Antoinette was happy now. If some querulousness had spoiled the harmony of her sweet voice, if some frowns had crossed her once smooth forehead, the jar in the tones and the frown of disappointed grief were quite gone, and it was again the bright gleeful little woman whom big

Stephen Le Breton had brought to make sunshine in his island home.

Proud and glad was she now to carry the little bundle of wrappings on her arm when she went to church on Sundays; proud was she too when she sat on the rocks with her treasure in her lap, and, the women pausing to look, said he was a "fine boy, and handsome." But I think the proudest and gladdest day to the little mother was when, on the third morning after his birth, her baby was laid in her arms by his happy father, with the words, "He is another *Stephen* for you, 'Toinette."

"God bless you, my baby, my Stephen!" prayed the earnest loving woman. "May the Virgin Mother and the saints watch over you, and keep you pure and spotless; may the blessed Saint Stephen, who died for the love of Christ, make you good and holy like himself."

Ah, yes, Antoinette, it is a heart-felt prayer, such as God will never reject, even if offered ignorantly and amiss.

Not Virgin Mother, not saints, not even Stephen, who died a martyr for God's truth, shall make thy little child pure, or keep him holy; but Jesus, who loves little ones, will watch over this baby and lead him into the fulness of light!

The young Stephen's babyhood was much like that of all other children; it was not till he was fully nine months old that any one began to think there was something strange about those large, black, unblinking eyes of his, which seemed to meet the hot glare of sunshine as easily as the tender glow of evening light.

"Nay, but there's a strange look in his eyes;" it was old Martha Vallère who said it first; poor old Martha, who, good as she certainly was, had the reputation of being ever the first to croak of evil.

"Strange!" exclaimed the proud little mother, snatching baby Stephen from under the old crone's close inspection, as if it could do him harm. "They are the sweetest eyes, the eyes of my own dear father away in la belle Normandie. What do you know of the eyes of a young baby, Mère Vallère?"

"I *ought* to know," said the old woman, nodding her head sagely. "There's a many babies I've had to do with, letting alone five of my own all lying in the churchyard, years and years gone back. Yes, Antoinette Le Breton, let me tell you I never saw that look in a baby's eyes but once, and then—"

"And then?" repeated the poor mother, passionately.

"Then they never were any use to him—he had been born blind."

It was a low cry, but oh how heart-broken, the cry which came from our poor Antoinette! Even deaf old Martha heard and was touched by it, and beginning to fear lest she had said too much, laid her trembing old hand on the younger woman's arm.

But Mrs. Le Breton shook her off, and drawing the baby's wrappings closer, ran up the shore towards the town, never heeding that she was in her home-dress—the short petticoat and high Norman cap and wooden sabots which she (proud little peasant!) liked to exchange for more English costume when she went into St. Helier, especially when she wished to get speech of the Père Guillaume.

Thither she sped now with rapid step, seeing nothing, hearing nothing, not even the salutations of friends who met her in the way and paused to look at her flying figure, wondering what was wrong. On, on, until she had passed the market-place, and so to the retired street where the presbytery or priest's house stood, close to his church.

Whatever of error was in the Père Guillaume's preaching, we must in justice own that he was a sincere man, honestly believing all which he had been trained from childhood to accept as truth. A kind man he was, too, to his flock, especially the poorest, or the most sorrowful, as the dirty ragged beggars who besieged his doorway might have testified, or as you might have learned in many a home to which he had been the only visitor in time of sorest need. To Père Guillaume little Mrs. Le Breton hurried now in her sudden terror; she almost believed that one so good could work a miracle, like such she had read of in the saints' lives, and restore her baby's sight, if, indeed, what old Martha hinted at was true.

But it was not, it *could not be.* How many times poor Antoinette assured herself of that during her hurried walk I could not tell you, nevertheless her heart beat nervously, and her face looked pale and anguished, as she dropped her curtsey to the priest.

"You are weary with that heavy boy of yours," said Père Guillaume, kindly; "seat yourself, mon enfant, and rest awhile."

Antoinette sunk on to one of the wooden chairs, but speech failed her; she only looked at the priest with wild imploring eyes.

"Mais, ma fille, what has happened?" questioned the father, in that mixture of French and English which he had fallen into the habit of using; "you have no care, no sorrow? Stephen, yourself, the little one, are well; is it not so?"

Then Antoinette rose, and held out her little Stephen. "Ah! mon père, mais dites-moi donc," she gasped; "ses yeux, his pretty eyes—there is nothing amiss!"

The priest gazed with puzzled face at

the little woman, and then at the baby, who lay cooing on her arm, with wide-open eyes as black as sloes.

"Ses yeux! Je ne comprends pas—I do not understand," he responded. "Why should there be anything to trouble you, my child, in the eyes of this innocent little one?"

Somewhat reassured by his words, Mrs. Le Breton told what had passed between herself and old Martha but just a little while before on the rocks, where she had been sitting with her darling. When she ceased speaking a deep silence fell upon them both; evidently the Père Guillaume was troubled.

"It might be; I never thought of it," he murmured; then raising his voice to its usual tone, he laid his hand gently on the mother's arm. "If this should indeed be so—if the good God sends you this cross, will you not try to bear it, my child?" he said.

Antoinette almost screamed. "Bear it! bear to see my boy, my darling, blind!" she cried. "That he should never look on the sunshine and the waves, never

THE BABY LAY COOING ON HER ARM.

know the face of his own mother; *how* could I bear it, Père Guillaume?"

"By prayer," said the priest, quietly. "Many and great have been the crosses borne by the saints, Antoinette; and yet they counted them as nothing in comparison with the crown which awaited them in heaven. Wilt thou not also bear the cross that thou mayest win the crown, my daughter?"

"No, no!" cried the mother, half unconscious what she said in her anguish of heart; "not this, not such a cross as this! Oh! mon père, you are good, you are holy, like the blessed saints of old; I pray you heal my little one, if, indeed, he is blind!"

The priest smiled sadly. "I am no saint, my child," he said. "Were it so, the good God might indeed use me as the humble instrument of bringing you miraculous aid. But the saints can help you now, though they are not in this world; to them you must address yourself, if, indeed, this cross is laid upon you. But perchance old Martha was wrong, Antoinette; shall we try to find if this is so?"

"Yes, yes, mon père!" exclaimed the mother, catching at the hope held out to her. She almost expected the priest to return with some relic which would of a certainty give sight by its touch; but he only brought a lighted candle.

Bidding Antoinette draw near the window, Père Guillaume passed the light close to the infant's eyes; it never shrunk. Again, and a third time; but the wide black eyes gazed on unflinchingly, not even was there a passing quiver of the lid. The priest set down his candle, and made the sign of benediction above the heads of both mother and child. "Que le bon Dieu soit votre consolation," he said, solemnly; and then Antoinette knew the terrible truth; knew that her baby, her one only darling, was hopelessly blind.

Bitterly she moaned; nay, she would have fallen, had not the priest set her in a chair. He would have taken the baby from her, but she held it in a tight straining clasp.

"Mon enfant—my Stephen," she murmured, in a low and sorrowful tone. "What hast thou done, sweet innocent, that God's punishment should fall on thee?" Then, after a gush of tears, "'Tis I who am the cause; my sins have brought this judgment from heaven on thee, my baby, and yet I would die for thee!"

Poor Antoinette! Oh, had there been but one to tell her that not in wrath, but in love—not in punishment, but in mercy, are these trials sent from heaven, some comfort might have crept into her heart, even in that saddest, darkest moment of her life. But such was not the teaching of her religion. Père Guillaume could tell only of the merit to be gained by trial bravely borne; of the pains of purgatory remitted by suffering in this world; of the sharp corrections our sins deserve even though One died that they may be forgiven. Such teaching gave no comfort, no rest to the poor stricken woman, who believed God was angry with her.

"I will go, I will take him home," she sobbed, rising; "I thank you, mon père, for I know you pity me. By-and-by, perhaps le bon Dieu will help me to be resigned, but I cannot yet."

"Ah! pauvre enfant," said the priest, kindly, "deep as is thy grief, it is but as nothing compared with that of Mary when she witnessed the sufferings of her Divine Son. She feels for thee now; she is pleading for thee, Antoinette, she who knows a mother's heart so well; call upon her, my child, cry to her 'Mater dolorissima, ora pro me.'"

Slowly, slowly, fell poor Antoinette's footsteps now; she hardly dared go home and face old Martha's questioning, and listen to the exclamations of pity and surprise which would pour out when the news once spread among the cottages near her own. But neither Martha nor Mrs. Le Fevre nor any other of the neighbours came across her path as she bore her treasure homewards; and gaining her door she entered, and barring it fast against all intruders laid little Stephen in his cradle, and then gave vent to her own terrible grief.

"Oh! Mater dolorissima, Mother of Sorrows, pray for me!" she whispered ever and again; yet no peace came, and Antoinette had never heard, or, if she had, had never heeded, the sweet words, "Come unto Me, all ye that labour and are heavy laden, and *I* will give you rest."

Meanwhile Père Guillaume had walked down the town to the carpenter's shed where Stephen Le Breton was busy at his work. Cheerily he sang over it—he was thinking of Joseph the carpenter at that very moment, and picturing the time when, just as the priest told him, Jesus had worked by His foster-father's side, his little Stephen should share his daily labour. A kind and compassionate heart had Père Guillaume, and now he paused outside the shed, half dreading to carry the sad news to this man who sang over his work with lightness of heart.

It was one of the hymns which recent years have introduced into the Catholic evening service, an English hymn, which fell in harmonious tones from Le Breton's lips:

> "There be many saints above,
> Who watch us with true love,
>   But Joseph, none like thee.
> Dearest of saints, be near us
> Whether we live or die."

"Always singing at thy work, friend Stephen," said the priest, entering.

The man removed his cap, and saluted Père Guillaume.

"Well, yes, father; it beguiles the time, and makes the work easier."

"Well, well—you could not do better, man; let your mind dwell on such good thoughts as those which find expression in your English hymns. The *cantiques* of France are beautiful, too, Stephen; you must have heard them often in the church near your Antoinette's home in Normandy."

"Ah, yes, father, and 'Toinette's voice can trill them like a bird; but mine—well, the English suits better."

"It is as I told thee, mon fils, is it not?" said the priest. "Thy 'Toinette makes thee a good and pious wife, like a true Norman maiden should?"

"Ah, yes, indeed, Père Guillaume, there's not my little woman's equal in the island; and since the good God bestowed on us the blessing we desired so long, none has a lighter heart than 'Toinette."

The priest sighed; "God is indeed a good and merciful Father," he said, as if thinking aloud. "None the less good when He corrects than when He favours us, Stephen. Do you know that, mon ami?"

"Yes, father, you have ever taught us so," responded Le Breton, quietly, little imagining the stroke which had fallen upon him and Antoinette.

"I have taught, but hast thou learned the lesson?" said the priest, gravely. "Nay—what am I saying?—not I, but God, shall be thy Teacher. Go to thy house, my son, and pray for grace to profit by the dealings of the Almighty."

Stephen paused in his work, and a look of dismay came across his usually placid face.

"To my home—is aught of trouble there?" he exclaimed, feeling for his working cap, as one stunned by some sudden shock.

In few words, but gentle ones, Père Guillaume told him the truth. Meanwhile Stephen's face paled and quivered like the face of a woman.

"My poor little one—my 'Toinette!" he murmured. "I must go to her. Ah, mon père, I thank you for breaking to me the tidings. I beseech your prayers;" and then the great strong man went out of the shed and into the street, but his step faltered, and he felt helpless as a child.

"Pauvres enfants," murmured the priest, looking after Stephen, "I will offer Mass for them to-morrow morning;" and he, too, went to his home.

## CHAPTER III.

Six years have gone by since we looked into the Le Bretons' cottage on the sea-shore; six years since Antoinette used to rock her first-born child to sleep to the music of the blue waves, which came rippling up so softly in the summer sunshine.

Three sturdy little ones now trot in and out of the low doorway, and a baby of a few weeks old lies in the old rocking cradle, tended by blind Stephen.

Merry rogues are they. Fifine, Antony, and Marie. Rosy and stout, with white teeth gleaming through their parted lips, and eyes black as eyes can be; just such eyes as Stephen's, but that they dance with light and intelligence, and his are lustreless.

Poor little boy! Many a Mass has been said for him; many a novena made—nay, Antoinette even went across to her Norman home, and thence with the child in her arms made a pilgrimage to the noted shrine of Notre Dame de la Délivrance, yet Stephen remains blind.

But surely of all the little ones he is the most dearly loved—none so dear to heart of father and of mother as their first-born son, whose wide-open black eyes look upon their faces, yet see not the tenderness and love with which those faces turn upon him.

A good, gentle boy is little six-year old Stephen. His mother tells proudly how helpful he is to her, how he tends the sleeping baby, rocking the cradle with his small fair hands—so unlike the strong, wilful little hands of the other children; how he can light the fire, and fetch water, and do ever so many things in the cottage, as well as if he was not blind.

Delicate the child may look, but he is not unhappy; how could he be, when so much love is poured out upon him? Tenderly he loves his father and the other children, but the depth of strong devotion in little Stephen's heart was certainly centred in his mother.

Antoinette is changed since we saw her last. A great deal of the sprightly beauty is gone, seldom does her laugh ring merrily through her cottage home, nor is her step so glad and swift as once it was. The sorrow which came with the knowledge of little Stephen's blindness has left its print upon her; but time has in part healed the wound, and outwardly, at least, Antoinette is resigned. The happiest time for mother and little son is when they are alone together. When baby Henri is sleeping in his cradle too soundly to need rocking—when Fifine, and Antony, and Marie are tucked snugly in their beds, or else have gone to play together by the edge of the waves, while Stephen sits with his mother, who watches them from the seat on the rocks.

Many a story does Antoinette tell the boy in these quiet moments—stories of some old saints, or quaint legends which please his dreaming, fanciful nature, and most often of all of Stephen, the first martyr, after whom he himself is named; but Martha Vallère, with her spectacles on her nose, reads it to the little blind boy from her old worn Bible.

A strange fancy had Stevie for the deaf old woman; when his mother was busy, yet did not need his small services, he would leave the children's merry play and steal softly into the next cottage, where, laying a tiny soft hand upon her brown wrinkled one, he would plead, "Martha, read me a Bible story."

Perhaps, had Père Guillaume understood the mixed nature of the little boy's religious training, he might have interposed; but the parents never thought to tell him. It was sufficient for them that Stevie was obedient, kind, and gentle; that he loved to say the prayers they taught him, and to go to the church in the town on Sundays, where the music seemed like heaven, he said. As for his visits to old Protestant Martha—why, Antoinette would have said she did no harm to the blind child; and who could object to anything which made him happy and contented?

So, all unconsciously, Stephen was learning truth which would never be forgotten, and seed was being sown which should bring forth a future harvest.

Well did he know the stories and legends of the saints his mother loved to tell of, but almost better did he know the stories of Christ's earthly life, which Martha read to him from the Bible; and best of all did he know and love the one which tells of him who also was blind, and who prayed, "Lord, that I may receive my sight," and was healed of his infirmity. With that intuitive delicacy which sensitive children possess, little Stephen felt that this was not a history to speak much of to his mother. Once he had begun, but tears streamed down her face (he felt them drop upon his own when she kissed him), and straining him to her breast she had cried, "Oh! my little son, my Stephen! would that that blessed One was here now! then would I walk the world over, bearing you in my arms, if He would give light to you also."

Stephen knew that for many days after

that conversation his mother was sad, so he spoke no more of it; yet the scene seemed to rest in his mind like a picture, and he begged old Martha to read to him of "Christ making the blind man to see," over and over again.

"Would He give sight to my eyes if He came here now?" questioned Stephen.

Martha was puzzled for a moment. "I can't rightly say, dearie. 'Tis likely He would, too, for He was always good and kind, yet perhaps He'd see 'twas best so; then He would leave you as you are, Stevie."

"Best so!" and Stevie's voice was grieved. "It can't be *best* never to see the waves, which mother tells me are now blue and gentle, now angry and large, as they break upon the rocks. Never to see the sun and the flowers, and little Marie and the rest, and mother's face. Oh, Martha, that *can't* be best!"

"We'll know by-and-by, when we get to heaven, dearie," said Martha, wiping her eyes. Little Stephen's love had made its way into her heart, and softened much which had once been hard and uncompromising in it. "Suppose you could see like other people, and left off liking to think of God and hear of Jesus, and didn't care to be a good boy to your mother, that would be worse than being blind, Stephen, wouldn't it?"

"Oh yes," said the child, promptly. "But Jesus made the blind man see, and I suppose he did not leave off loving Jesus. Surely he could not when He had healed him. Do you think Christ Jesus loves me best blind, Martha?"

"Ay, sure He does, my boy, or He wouldn't have let it be," said Martha, decidedly; and from that day little Stephen Le Breton never wished again to receive his sight.

As time went on the blind boy learned many a little useful art which kept him happy and employed. One taught him to make fishing-nets, another to plait straw; and when summer time brought visitors to the island, there were few among them who did not make acquaintance with the little sightless fellow, with black lustreless eyes, who sat among his brothers and sisters at the cottage door, and served as a sort of small guard upon them, or at any rate as a peace-maker when they quarrelled, as they played on the sand or scrambled about the rocks.

It was thus that Stephen heard of skilful doctors who could sometimes restore sight; but he never wished to go to them, for had not Martha assured him that the Lord Jesus loved him best as he was? Some one spoke of cure to Antoinette; even offered to be at the expense of a trial, but she indignantly refused—if St. Lucy, the special patron of the blind, had not cured her boy, if the Blessed Virgin had not granted the request, to make which she had gone on pilgrimage, it was not possible that doctors could do anything—so said Mrs. Le Breton.

When these well-meaning visitors spoke to her of schools for the teaching of the blind, where Stephen could learn to read, she was only a shade less angry. How should she part with her boy, her first-born son, to go across the rough sea to England? She said, "No; Stevie was good and happy, the comfort and blessing of his father and mother, and, thanking the ladies, she wanted nothing more."

But Père Guillaume could have told how the passing years had done little towards assuaging Antoinette's grief, how many a prayer and penance had been offered to Heaven for Stephen's healing, yet always in vain.

If no earthly ray of sunlight had penetrated the darkness in which Stevie's life was passed, gleams of heavenly light had already been sent to him; and he had learned, what his mother was blind to understand, that if Jesus Christ had chosen his sightlessness for him, it was best so, better far than to see with the eyes, and yet be spiritually blind to the love and beauty and tenderness of the Saviour.

But Stephen was not only loved and loving in his home; there was not one among the neighbours, not one of the townspeople, who did not know the blind boy, and show him many a kindness. It was pretty to see his bright little face in one of the heavy market-carts which made their way early on Saturday mornings from the outlying country parts to St. Helier. Either old Mrs. Le Fevre fancied she needed his clever little fingers in unpacking her chickens and butter, or Mrs. Le Maistre was passing, and thought the drive would amuse him; and so one and another of the Jersey folks found some reason for pausing at the door of Le Breton's cottage and borrowing Stevie from his mother.

Many a time Antoinette would make time enough to run up to the market, not so much to purchase, as to see her little son with one or other of his friends, and, coming home, would tell with pride how English ladies had talked with him, and officers patted him on the head; and once the Governor of the island was there, and condescended to listen as Nannette at the flower-stall told Stephen's little tale. Yes, every one loved Stephen, the blind child whose birth had been such a joy to big Stephen and his wife 'Toinette, and whose affliction had brought sorrow upon all who knew the parents.

So time rolled by, and Stevie was growing a good-sized boy. Père Guillaume began to think of the time when he should make his first communion, and therefore bade Antoinette send him twice each week

HV2345
.R34
1882

The Blind
Boy of the
Island

to the church, where a class of boys were also to receive the necessary instruction. Stephen made no objection to this, he had even been willing to repeat his catechism to his mother; but the priest's teaching had not for him the charm of old Martha's Bible reading, and he would run all the more eagerly to her after the catechising, begging for one of the best-loved stories.

Now and then, when Père Guillaume walked down to the shore to visit such of his flock as were neighbours of the Le Bretons, he found Stephen sitting on the rocks gazing as steadily out to sea as if his eyes could behold the waves on the distant horizon.

"Of what do you think, here alone?" said the priest, to him once; but he did not expect the ready reply:

"I am thinking of our Lord Jesus, mon père, when He walked upon the waves, and His disciples were affrighted until He spoke, and said to them, 'It is I, be not afraid.'"

"Yes, it is a beautiful picture to have in the mind as one sits by the sea-shore, my child," replied Père Guillaume, gazing wonderingly at Stephen. "Our Lord did marvellous things, and so also have the holy saints. Did you ever hear of him who though but a boy, being commanded by his master to run to the aid of a companion who had fallen into the water, passed across its surface as if it had been dry land? It was the reward of his prompt obedience."

Stephen looked doubtful. "I never heard *that*," he said; but now a light passed over his face as he added, "I like better to hear of Christ doing wonderful things. I like the story of when He was asleep in the boat, and a great storm rose up, and the disciples cried out, and then He rose up and bade the winds and waves be calm. I often think of that when I lie in bed and listen to the storms which come sometimes. I tell it to Fifine and Antony, and then they do not cry."

Père Guillaume passed on after a few more words, but he was not quite satisfied about Stephen. It was well that he should know the miracles of Christ, but not better than the lives of saints; besides, how had he heard of these things? The priest went into Mrs. Le Breton's home to inquire about it.

Antoinette had a good report to give of Stephen; he was always the best of her children, the most gentle, obedient, and pious, so she told Père Guillaume. "And how did he occupy himself?" Well, he minded the younger ones, and did little services in the house, and then for amusement he would never weary of sitting on the shore, unless he ran to the next cottage, where an old woman—poor Martha Vallère—told him tales of which he never seemed to get enough, wonderful tales of the blessed Christ when He was in the world.

That was all Antoinette Le Breton had to tell; but the priest turned it over in his mind during his walk home, and decided that those conversations and visits must be watched over, and, if necessary, put a stop to.

## CHAPTER IV.

THOSE who know the little island which is the scene of my story, know also the sweet and peaceful Val des Vaux, but a short distance removed from the life and bustle of the town. A few—a very few—picturesque dwellings may be found there, but they lie in the hollow, and on each side rises the high hill, or côtil, as in Jersey patois it is called, while a little trickling stream winds through the vale, from which the cattle drink as they come with tinkling bells from the higher ground. A favourite walk was this with Stephen Le Breton on a Sunday afternoon, when he would take the elder children out of Antoinette's way for an hour or two, and watch them picking flowers, which they floated on the rippling stream. It was on one such Sunday that blind Stephen heard words which sunk deeply into his heart, never, never to leave it more—the first time he had ever heard the plain and simple story of the Saviour's redeeming love.

It was only a poor man telling God's message to some dozen or more men, women, and children; but it came from his *heart*, and thus it appealed to the hearts of those who heard. Le Breton was resting on the green sward some way off; the children were playing, all but little blind Stephen, who, hearing a voice, and catching a familiar word or two, went forward and gave eager, breathless attention. "Whosoever believeth in Him shall not perish"—those were the words which rang ever in the little boy's ears after that Sunday afternoon; and he understood that it was Jesus, the Christ who stilled the storm, in whom to believe was to have everlasting life. There was something very pleasant in such tidings to Stephen, for since he had been going to Père

Guillaume's weekly classes he had begun to think more of how to save his soul, and, according to the priest's teaching, it was indeed a difficult matter. First of all there was the terrible "mortal sin" to be avoided—sin that would plunge the soul into endless torment. And then the "venial sins"—the sins and faults of every day, which none but the saints could ever hope to be free from, yet for every one of which there was such suffering in purgatory. Stephen often felt very troubled when he had been hearing of these things. It was true that Père Guillaume told them that God's grace, conveyed by the holy sacraments of the Church, would save their souls, but purgatory was certain, and the little boy trembled when it was pictured to him.

But now in the peaceful sun-lit valley he heard a different message; and then, as it was out of the Bible, the very words of Christ the Son of God, surely, *surely* it must be true. No talk of hard penances and austerities; no invention of fasts and pilgrimages, of Mass or sacraments, only that "*whosoever* believeth" shall not perish.

Stephen felt as if he should like to run and tell all his friends that happy news. Surely even Père Guillaume did not know it, or he need not mortify himself as much as people whispered of, he need not tell little children how they would have to suffer in the fires of purgatory. Perhaps the little boy would have ventured on carrying what he had learned to the priest, but for the check he received from his own father.

It was when the preacher had disappeared, and the little knot of listeners gone their several ways, that the blind child had seated himself by big Stephen and put his small hand in the large brown one.

"Where has my boy been all this while?" asked Le Breton in the caressing tone he always used to his afflicted child; and Stephen told him eagerly.

To his surprise, his father became vexed with him.

"The Père Guillaume would scold you well if he saw you listening to that heretic fellow, Stephen," said he. "You—a boy preparing for your first communion too, to be so taken with such words. Never do it again, child."

It was the first time that Le Breton had ever spoken sternly to his little boy; and Stephen could not recover himself even when he was back in the cottage and at his mother's side.

"What ails the child?" said Antoinette to her husband; and Le Breton told her.

"He is so young, so innocent, he knew no harm!" she exclaimed. "You should not have spoken harshly to him, Stephen;" and then she had taken her child apart, and told him not to grieve, for his father was not really angry, he knew that his little Stephen had not understood he was doing wrong.

"Wrong! to listen to the words of God, mother?" repeated the boy; and Antoinette, puzzled how to answer him, kissed his sad face and said it was only wrong to listen to any other teacher than their priest, the good Père Guillaume.

Stephen said no more, but he thought much of all this, and a troubled look came often on his face, which had been once so calm and peaceful. And another sorrow followed—they seldom come singly in the lives of any one of us—for his old friend Martha was found dead in her bed one Sunday morning, when one of the neighbours, seeing no smoke rising from her cottage chimney, went in to inquire. No more Bible stories for blind Stephen now. Père Guillaume was glad when he heard of it—for the good of the child's soul, as he said; but Mrs. Le Breton in her own mind regretted very sincerely that her boy had lost the visits, which had been a strange happiness to him from his babyhood.

After the first burst of childish grief, however, he was very patient, though he talked less than before, even to his mother, and crept off to the shore whenever he was not likely to be missed, where he thought of his favourite stories, and said over to himself the verses Martha had taught him from her old Bible.

He grew so thin and feeble at that time that the watchful mother considered it impossible for him to keep up his attendance at Père Guillaume's classes; the walk was too long, she said; and though his first communion should be put off for another year, the child was still so young, perhaps it was better so.

Stephen did not feel sorry to hear this. Sometimes he thought he must indeed be a bad boy, not to desire the first communion day more, to which the other Catholic children looked forward as to the great event of their lives; but then the truth was that the simple doctrine of faith and love had rooted itself so strongly in the child's heart that the other harder and more complicated scheme of salvation had no attraction for him. To Stephen Le Breton it was happiness to sit by the shore and think of Christ in the fisherman's boat; Christ raising the dead, healing the sick, giving sight to the blind. When he went to his church, and knew that amidst light and incense and flowers there was a little place in the altar where Christ was said to dwell, his heart did not respond to it, and he felt glad to get out into the street and away to his quiet home and his quiet thoughts.

We have already said that since the pilgrimage to the far-famed shrine, Antoinette had given up all thought of cure for her blind boy; they had ceased to speak of such a thing as possible; and the child himself appeared perfectly content with his lot. But in the autumn following upon old Martha Vallère's death Mrs. Le Breton came home from church one evening in a state of unusual preoccupation. Père Guillaume had been speaking to his people of Lourdes, where was a well of miraculous water, which had already cured the blind, the lame, and those who were sick with many and terrible diseases.

Antoinette had been, as she thought, inspired from heaven with the certainty that if only her boy could go to drink of that miraculous fountain, to bathe his poor sightless eyes with its clear waters, he would indeed be healed. She told her thought first to her husband as he was busy one evening nailing up the vine to the wall of the cottage; he stopped short, took the nails from his mouth, where he had put them for safe keeping, and gave a long low surprised whistle.

"So far away, to Lourdes; it is impossible, 'Toinette! Were we noble and rich, our Stephen might indeed travel to that wonderful place, but for us working folk such things cannot be."

But Mrs. Le Breton was not at all discouraged in her project, for the Père Guillaume had described the crowd of people who gathered daily by the miraculous stream; not only the rich, who were drawn there from devotion, but the poor also, who had journeyed far to be healed by the water whose fame spread continually throughout the Catholic world.

"I will talk to the good père," she said; and, accordingly, the next day, having a leisure hour, Antoinette walked into the town and called upon the priest.

After she had told him her errand, and enlarged upon what she considered an inspiration from above, there was a short silence, during which the Père Guillaume appeared to be thinking deeply.

"I will think over your pious project, my daughter," he said; "you will do well in the meantime to pray daily to the Holy Ghost for light to know the will of God in this matter. What does the child himself think of it?"

Mrs. Le Breton explained that she had deemed it better not to speak to Stephen until she had first consulted le bon père; he was too good and too pious a boy not to undertake the pilgrimage with joy, she said, if Père Guillaume counselled it.

The priest himself did not feel so sure upon this point; he had never felt perfect confidence in little Stephen since he discovered his love for Protestant Martha, and her stories from the Bible.

"Speak to him, ma fille," he said, at length; "relate to him the story of the miraculous water of Lourdes, and if his young heart is inspired with devotion and a lively faith, it may indeed be a heavenly inspiration which has been given you."

Mrs. Le Breton went home with renewed hope, and that evening when she sat at her sewing, with all the children round her, she told them the story of Lourdes, pretty much as she had heard it from the lips of the Père Guillaume.

"Tell us some story," little Marie had said.

"Yes, of the good fairies," suggested Fifine.

But the mother would tell no fairy story that night.

"Then tell us of the saint who carried bread in her cloak to feed the poor, and when she met her husband riding among his courtiers, the bread changed to roses, so that he might not be angry with her," said Antony.

"The dear Saint Elizabeth, you mean," replied Mrs. Le Breton. "Suppose, instead of telling you of her, I speak to you of what the good Père Guillaume spoke about in church but a few nights ago; something, I think, you have never before heard."

"Is it pretty?" cried Fifine, looking doubtful. "Is it the story of a child?"

"Yes, of a good and holy child named Bernadette," replied Antoinette; and as the general wish seemed now to hear this proposed story, and the merry voices were hushed to silence, the mother began to tell her children the story of the miraculous water of Lourdes.

"Once upon a time," began Mrs. Le Breton; but here Antony interrupted by asking if it was a long time ago.

"Peace, peace, child!" said Antoinette, reprovingly; "it was not so the good father was interrupted at church, nor will I suffer you to interrupt me when I tell you the same holy story."

Antony looked somewhat abashed, and as the rest grew increasingly serious under such an unusually sharp rebuke, Mrs. Le Breton began once more.

"In a little village of the south of France, my own dear country," she said, "there was dwelling a humble family, who were both honest and pious folk. Lourdes was the name of the little town, away in the Hautes Pyrenées, and all who dwelt there knew Bernadette, one of this good family, a child of still tender years." Here Mrs. Le Breton paused; but as no one, not even the talkative Antony, had a word to say, but were listening with rapt attention, she went on. "This little girl loved to pray, and as she watched over her sheep she would take her beads and say on them the rosary of the Blessed Virgin. She used to go to a grotto in the rocks to pray, and kneeling there one day she suddenly beheld a vision—the beautiful vision of a lady clothed in white, reciting the beads also, like herself. Bernadette felt afraid; but so sweet, so kind was the face of the vision, that her young heart grew peaceful and happy; and when at last it vanished from her sight, the child went home and told her parents what she had seen. They did not believe her story; they said it was but fancy. Again and again did Bernadette see the beauteous lady standing smiling in the rocky cave, yet no one else was privileged to see also, and thus none believed her simple tale."

"Perhaps she did fancy it, mother," suggested Antony. "I, too, think at night some one has come into the room, and I scream out, but Stevie tells me it is fancy."

"Naughty child!" exclaimed Antoinette. "Will you dare to speak of your fancies, when I am telling you the story of Lourdes, and the miraculous appearance of the Blessed Mary?" And, in spite of the boy's entreaties, he was carried to bed; and the rest of the story was postponed until some other time.

"Do you like this tale, Stevie?" asked Marie of her blind brother.

Stephen's face was troubled, and he lowered his voice: "I like best to hear stories of Christ Jesus," he said. "I do not want to vex mother, but, like Antony, I too think that Bernadette fancied she saw this vision."

## CHAPTER V.

IT was some days before Mrs. Le Breton would consent to continue the story she had begun. Being a strict Catholic, nothing was so likely to call forth her severity as any doubt of what was taught by the priest; and if Père Guillaume had described the marvels of Lourdes, Antony was a wicked boy to name his own childish fancies in proof that the pious little shepherdess was perhaps mistaken in what she declared true; in fact, Antoinette was a little troubled also by seeing Stephen's want of interest in her story, when her one strong desire was to excite in him such faith that he might go to the miraculous fountain and there be cured of his blindness,

However, when a week had passed, and it was Sunday evening, the children prevailed on their mother to continue the story, promising good behaviour.

"Where did I leave off, Stevie?" she asked her eldest boy.

"At where they did not believe what Bernadette told them," was the prompt reply; and its tone made Antoinette sigh.

"Ah, yes," she said. "There are those whose hearts are hard and dark; and even now, when so many miracles are wrought, they refuse to believe. Well, my children, Bernadette had seen the Blessed Mary many a time before even the good curé believed her story. But one day, as she knelt and prayed, the vision bade her approach and drink of the fountain. Bernadette knew well that no stream ran there, it was a dry and barren spot; so rising from her knees she was going away to drink of the river, when the Blessed Virgin called her once more. 'Drink of the fountain,' she said in silvery tones, and pointing to a corner near to where she stood. The child gazed; yes! there was indeed a little fountain of clear water gushing from the rock; and having drunk of it she went to the curé and told him what had happened. He hastened to the spot; a crowd gathered there, and they indeed beheld the fountain of which the little maiden had spoken; and they could no longer refuse belief."

Mrs. Le Breton looked round upon her children with an air of triumph, as if this was proof which none could doubt; she marvelled that Stephen still had a sad expression on his gentle face.

"I cannot now tell you one half of the wonders which have since been wrought by the miraculous water of Lourdes," said Antoinette. "Pilgrims from all parts have knelt there, some blind, some lame, some weak, and drinking the water have been immediately healed."

"Every one of them, mother?" put in Fifine.

Mrs. Le Breton hesitated. 'No, my child, I cannot say that there have been none who left no better than they came. Perhaps their faith was not strong and fervent, or perhaps the Virgin knew it was not for their welfare to grant her aid; how that may be I cannot tell. But listen, Fifine, and you also, my Stephen, to the first miracle worked after the water sprang from the rock. There was a poor man dwelling near Lourdes whose sight was gradually leaving him, until with one eye he could distinguish nothing. This unfortunate being heard of the miracle. 'Bring me the water!' he cried. 'If the Virgin sent it, I am sure it will have power to heal me.'

"The water was brought in a small glass; this man, whose faith was great, began to pray, and then dipping his finger into the water rubbed his sightless eye."

Here Antony's excitement burst forth. "And was he cured, mother?" cried he.

"Quite cured; and from that hour he saw with both eyes perfectly, and was again able to work for his living," replied Mrs. Le Breton, with great seriousness; and so the story ended.

The children talked it over among themselves, as children will; but whatever were their opinions, they took care not to incur their mother's anger by speaking of any doubt they might have on the subject; but blind Stephen stole away by himself, nor did his mother see him again till the others were in bed, and then she unfolded her scheme.

"You grow a great boy, my Stevie," she said, passing her hand fondly over his soft hair. "Would that you could see as other boys!"

"Oh, mother, I am quite happy," replied Stephen, quickly; "I used to mind about it sometimes when I was little, when I wanted to see the flowers, and the sunshine, and the waves, and you, mother. But now—" and he hesitated, while a light broke out over his face.

"But now?" questioned Antoinette. "Surely, my child, you would like the blessed gift of sight?"

"I do not know, mother," said the boy, quietly; "sometimes I think I like better to be just your blind Stevie. Sometimes, indeed, I think, if Christ Jesus was here, I should hardly ask Him to give me my sight; I should only want Him to put His hands on me and bless me."

Mrs. Le Breton looked anxiously at Stephen; it was plain to her that they did not think alike upon the subject.

"But, Stevie, my child, if you could go to this holy place, Lourdes, and pray to Mary, the Mother of Mercy, it may be that she would grant our petition, and the water of that fountain would be the means of your healing."

"Oh, mother, no, I cannot!" said the boy, shrinking.

"But think, my darling, of what it would be to see this beautiful world, the faces of your brothers and sisters, your parents, our home. You would like that, Stephen?"

"The water of that fountain will not do that for me, mother," said the child; "I do not wish to think of it, and I will wait for my sight till our Lord takes me to heaven."

"But if I, if the Père Guillaume wish you to undertake this pilgrimage, you must obey, Stephen," said the mother, gravely; "you are a child, and cannot judge of these things."

Stephen answered nothing, and soon after went away to bed, feeling as if there was a cloud creeping up between him and the mother he so dearly loved.

Nor was Antoinette at ease, she wondered if any harm had been done to the boy by heretic neighbours; all the priest's warnings concerning old Martha Vallère rushed back upon her mind now; and most heartily she wished that she could carry Stephen and all her children to her old French home, where they would be surrounded always by those of their own religion. In the little village in Normandy, they were all good Catholics, said Mrs. Le Breton to herself, just as her husband came into the kitchen.

"Is that the boy singing?" said he, smiling, and opening the door which led to the sleeping rooms, while Antoinette approached to listen.

Yes, it was Stephen, who had inherited his father's love of music. In a low voice, as if fearful of arousing the other children, he sang now one of the hymns he had picked up from some neighbour, and clearly the words came out:

> "There is a green hill far away,
>     Without a city wall,
>   Where the dear Lord was crucified,
>     Who died to save us all.

> We may not know, we cannot tell
>   What pains He had to bear;
> But we believe it was for us
>   He died and suffered there.
>
> He died that we might be forgiven,
>   He died to make us good;
> That we at last might go to heaven,
>   Saved by His precious blood."

Then the singing ended; but a look of dismay rather than of vexation passed between husband and wife.

"'Tis some Protestant hymn he has heard," said Le Breton between his teeth. "Antoinette, you must look well to the child; he does not understand rightly the harm he may do to his soul."

But Mrs. Le Breton was not going to admit her own fears.

"Bah! Stephen," she said, with her own French gesture of dissent. "Soyez tranquille; the boy is good, and his little hymns will do no harm, though, indeed, I myself would like to hear better those which our own holy Church approves. But soon, Stephen, I will take him across to Normandy; and after a little 'bon jour' to my father and mother we will journey to the south, and bathe his poor eyes at the fountain of Notre Dame de Lourdes. What shall you say when I bring him back healed?"

"Oh, what shall I *not* say in gratitude to the Blessed Virgin!" replied Le Breton, fervently. "God forbid that I should doubt; and yet it seems as if that would be a greater blessing than we merit, 'Toinette."

"Well, I don't know about that," said Mrs. Le Breton, frankly; she was not so humble as Stephen. "I am sure Père Guillaume could tell the many good works I have done, and penances too, to say nothing of paying for many a Mass, and all that the child might have his sight. He is eleven years and more now, and it seems to me that it is time Notre Dame heard our petitions."

"Ah, but if you have done good works think whether they have not been marred, perhaps, whatever the intention."

"Supper is ready," said Antoinette, who did not want to have her hopes discouraged. "We will speak of that, mon ami, when I bring your son with sight as clear as that of Marie or Fifine."

"God grant it!" murmured Le Breton; then he ate his supper in peace.

It soon became noised abroad among the neighbours that Antoinette was going to start for Lourdes with blind Stephen, and the excitement ran high. Her fellow Catholics commended her devotion, and promised prayers, Masses, and rosaries for the travellers. The Protestants, who certainly are most numerous in the island, laughed at such a wild scheme.

"Stay quietly in your home, 'Toinette, and resign yourself to the will of God," said Mrs. Le Maistre; but the fiery little woman, turning, closed her door to such "heretic talk."

"Well, I am sorry to hear it, very," said another; "but I will give an eye to the children, and help them if they are in perplexity."

Antoinette could but express herself obliged, though it was with some pride she added that, "Fifine was growing a great girl now, and could manage well; besides, the father was handy, not like some poor shiftless men she could name."

So, finding Mrs. Le Breton averse to

much talking over her plan, whatever the neighbours had to say was said to the boy.

"Do you think you'll get your sight away in that place, I can't rightly remember the name of?" asked old Mrs. Le Fevre, as they jolted along in the lumbering cart to market one Saturday.

"No, I shall never see till I get to heaven," said Stephen, quietly. "I go because it is my mother's will; and God has commanded children to 'obey their parents.'"

"You must pray much to la Sainte Vierge," said his friend Nannette, the French girl who sat at the flower-stall; "you will come back then and look at my bouquets, and tell me they are beautiful."

But Stephen only shook his head. "I pray to God every day," he said, "but I do not ask Him for my sight."

At length the day came when Mrs. Le Breton and Stephen left the sea-side cottage, and, crossing to St. Malo, soon reached the village where Stephen's grandparents lived, while Fifine, Marie, Antony, and little Henri remained at home in their father's care, talking constantly of all they would do when their brother came back.

"We must take him to the prettiest places, father," said Marie. "True, he has been there with us, but he has never seen with his own eyes how beautiful our island is. Oh, how happy we shall be!"

And Le Breton would echo, "Yes, how happy we shall be!" and yet there was not a shadow of hope in his heart.

So much did he reproach himself for this "want of faith," as he deemed it, that at last he sought counsel of Père Guillaume.

"Pray much," said the priest, when he had heard the doubt and foreboding which oppressed Le Breton. "Try to strengthen your devotion to the Virgin Mother by Masses heard in her honour, by offerings of candles and flowers at her altar, and then——"

"Yes, father," said the poor man, eagerly, "and then she will grant my request."

"I cannot tell; it may be so," was the answer. "We are all in the hands of God."

So Stephen Le Breton went to his home little comforted. Meantime, Antoinette wrote cheerfully from Normandy. Others from the village were going with them, she said; there would be quite a little band of pilgrims to the fountain in the grotto of Lourdes, "and fear not, Stephen, for each day we hear of fresh miracles worked there."

## CHAPTER VI.

ALL this time little Stephen was quietly obedient to what his mother forced on him; but never could he be induced to display the slightest faith in the healing which was so talked of, nor would he say rosaries like the rest.

"I love to think Christ Jesus is near me, and I am telling Him all I want," he said; and as his mother was puzzled at such words she left him to his own course, so long as he submitted in the matter of the pilgrimage.

He used to comfort himself more than ever now with the stores of texts with which old Martha Vallère had stored his mind. Poor old Martha! in spite of a rough exterior and a naturally discontented spirit, she had cherished a true love of God and faith in Jesus Christ, and had been the instrument in implanting some of that faith and love in the heart of the blind child.

The verses Stephen liked best were those which spoke most plainly of the work of the Saviour. "Thou wast slain, and hast redeemed us to God by Thy blood," he would whisper to himself as he walked by his mother's side to church, or "Who loved me, and gave Himself for me," "Suffer little children to come unto Me," and others which he had learned in Martha's cottage.

Antoinette observed that his voice was silent during the singing of the *cantiques* in praise of Mary; but she tried to believe this was because he was accustomed to English hymns; she could not yet bring herself to suppose there was any other reason. If his faith was not as firm and strong as she desired, it was her own fault, her carelessness in letting him be so much in the society of old Martha, not heeding the warnings of the Père Guillaume.

By-and-by all would be well; once cured by the miraculous water, Stephen would be full of love and gratitude to the Blessed Virgin—there was no doubt of it! But first of all they must stay a little with the old people, who might not live much longer, perhaps, and who were so happy to have their daughter and their son in the little Norman home.

One day Antoinette found Stephen describing to his grandfather and some of the villagers the scenes he loved best to dwell on in the life of Christ; they were listening entranced and astonished.

"Ah, how learned he is!" exclaimed the simple folk, raising their hands. "Doubtless when he is a man he will be a priest, like monsieur le curé."

Another time she heard him singing to his old grandmother a hymn which he had not learned in the church of the Père Guillaume:

> "Jesus, refuge of my soul,
>   Let me to Thy bosom fly."

"Peace, child!" cried Mrs. Le Breton, hurrying in. "It is a hymn of the heretic children of Jersey! what would happen should monsieur le curé be passing by?"

But the old grandmother did not approve of the interruption; she had not understood one word, but she liked to hear Stephen's voice, and so called him to sing to her whenever she felt they were sure of being by themselves.

At length, however, the pilgrimage must be undertaken, for many miles had to be traversed before Antoinette should have her heart's desire.

It was early one May morning that she started with Stephen and some eight or ten of the villagers who were glad to join the pilgrimage, while those who remained at home came out to bid them adieu, and many even accompanied them on the first two or three miles of the journey.

Although all the distance was not to be accomplished on foot, there was much weary toiling up steep paths and down ravines before they arrived at Lourdes. When the town was reached the little company formed themselves in procession, one carrying a banner before them and singing the "Litany of the Blessed Virgin

LOURDES.

Mary," reached the far-famed grotto, and kneeling, drank of its waters.

How shall I describe the prayers of poor Antoinette; the hope, the faith, and then the bitter sickening disappointment as at last she was convinced that all was vain? Again and again had Stephen drunk of the miraculous fountain; again and again were its waters poured upon his sightless eyes, while friends looked on confident that he would be healed.

At last a sorrowful little company toiled back to peaceful Normandy, forced to admit that no cure had been made by the powerful Notre Dame de Lourdes.

Only the boy himself was light of heart; he could not be disappointed, for he had never hoped for sight to be given.

In obedience to his mother's will he had indeed drunk of the far-famed spring, and suffered his eyes to be bathed as often as it pleased her; but a little verse he heard often in his own island home seemed always in his mind at such times, so that he could hardly refrain from singing it aloud:

"I heard the voice of Jesus say,
  'Behold, I freely give
The living water; thirsty one,
  Stoop down, and drink, and live.'
I came to Jesus, and I drank
  Of that life-giving stream;
My thirst was quenched, my soul revived,
  And now I live in Him."

The boy did not fully understand it; he used often to wish he had some one to explain what it was to "live in Jesus;" but the lines pleased him, for he felt that if indeed the sweet voice of Christ spoke to him like that, oh! he would be glad to go to Him and drink water which gave peace and light and life.

The evening before they left Lourdes, Stephen was sitting alone a little way from the grotto where his mother prayed. Poor woman, she was bemoaning the sins by reason of which she believed her petition had not been granted her!

As he sat there he was singing softly one of his little hymns, when a pleasant voice spoke quite close to him and said, "Do you know the words of that hymn, my boy?"

"If you please I can't see who it is; I am blind," said Stephen.

After a few more words he found he was talking to an English lady, who soon won from him his story, and how he had come to Lourdes because his mother thought the water would heal him. He further added that he had not expected it himself; and a few questions from his new friend drew out the fact that though a Catholic by birth and training, Stephen Le Breton was full of simple love to the Saviour, and full too of desire to understand more of the way of salvation.

"I heard a man preach in our own island," he added. "It was in the Val des Vaux, and father was angry with me for listening, but I never forgot the words I heard: 'Whosoever believeth in Him shall not perish.'"

"And do you believe in Christ?" asked this lady. "Do you think you are one of His own children?"

Stephen seemed a little puzzled, but he brightened up as his companion told him simply of the Lord Jesus Christ, what it was to have faith in Him, love to Him, to strive to follow His example, and, thus living, to hope for pardon and salvation through His atonement made on Calvary.

"I think I try to please Him," said Stephen, gently; "I know I pray to Him, and ask Him to make me good, and to forgive me all my sins."

And then the lady told him how she had come to Lourdes on purpose to try and find an opportunity of speaking to some poor weary one who did not know that Christ had ever said, "Come unto Me, all ye that labour and are heavy laden, and I will give you rest;" some one perhaps cast down beneath a sense of sin, who did not know that Christ had said, "Thy sins and thy iniquities I will remember no more," or one who, drinking of the water, had thought to be healed, yet had never been taught to ask for that "living water" which they who drink shall never thirst again.

"That reminds me of the hymn I like so much!" cried Stephen; and he repeated the lines he had sung so often to himself at Lourdes:

"I heard the voice of Jesus say,
 'Behold, I freely give
The living water; thirsty one,
 Stoop down, and drink, and live.'"

The lady talked a little more to the boy, explaining to him what was that thirst after light, after peace, after pardon, which Jesus alone could satisfy, as water quenched our natural thirst; and how they who thus came in humble faith to Christ begin to "live in Him."

They were still speaking when Mrs. Le Breton came up to take Stephen away; and the lady explained that she had been interested in him and hoped to see him again.

But Antoinette's replies were short, and it was plain that she was not pleased. They were starting homeward the next day, she said, and Stephen would not be at the grotto any more.

"Then good-bye, my dear little boy," said his new acquaintance; "I hope one day we shall see each other in heaven."

"It's fine work talking of heaven!" muttered Antoinette, as she turned away. "Those sort of people don't seem to understand that it's hard work getting in there."

Stephen said nothing, but in his own heart there was a happy restful knowledge that there was One who made it easy; One who only asks our faith and love, and then He will pardon every sin and take us when we die to the Father's house of many mansions, which is prepared for all who love Him.

Away in the little cottage by the shore there was more of sorrow than of joy in thinking of Stephen's return, for was he not coming blind as he had left? Fifine, Marie, and Antony were loudly expressing their surprise that Notre Dame de Lourdes had not healed their brother.

"I think she is not so kind, after all," said little Henri; but his father reproved him.

"We must be resigned to the will of God, my children," he said. "It was not His will that the water of Lourdes should cure our Stephen, as it cured so many others who go on pilgrimage there."

"But why?" asked the children; and Le Breton could only shake his head and leave them to talk it out among themselves.

"Stevie is coming home, but he can't see," they told the neighbours; and so from one to another the news spread that poor Antoinette's long journey had been fruitless, and she was returning disappointed after all her hopes and prayers.

"I pity her," said old Madame Le Fevre; "she has been brought up in all this superstition, so that she believes it from the bottom of her heart; but as for Stevie, I think it is a different matter. I remember only the last Saturday I took him to the market, and we were talking together, he turned his face towards me and said, "I shall never see till I get to heaven."

"Yes," rejoined another of the group, who were talking together. "Stevie is quite different to the rest of them. I often spoke to him when I saw him sitting alone on the rocks, and now and then I'd ask him what he was thinking of. 'Of Christ walking on the sea,' he would say sometimes; or perhaps it was of Christ blessing the children, or carrying the cross up Calvary; but it was always of Christ, and not of the Virgin or the saints. Depend on it that boy is one of God's children."

And so in talking over Stephen's home-coming every one had something kind to say of the boy; and when the day came on which Antoinette brought him home many of the women were there to meet them.

"Cheer up, 'Toinette," said one; "your blind boy is better than many a son who has his sight, for he is good and dutiful."

But Mrs. Le Breton burst into tears, and shut the door upon them all, for her heart was too full to speak. She had expected so firmly to come home triumphing in Stephen's cure, that every word, even kindly meant, seemed like a mockery to her in her grief.

"Oh, Mary, pray for us who have recourse to thee!" she murmured that night as she knelt before the image of the Virgin; and while she thus prayed with sorrowing heart and fast-falling tears, little Stephen slept peacefully, for his last thought had been of Him who said, "Whatsoever ye shall ask the Father in My name, He will give it you." The blind boy had asked in the name of Jesus, not, indeed, the physical sight which had been denied him, but that which should enable him to see the way of salvation; to understand all Christ had done and suffered to redeem his soul from death and hell; and his prayer had been answered, he had become a little follower and servant of the Great Master, and thus he was content.

## CHAPTER VII.

AFTER the first disappointment and sorrow had spent itself, things went on much the same in Mrs. Le Breton's cottage as they had done before the journey to Lourdes. The only change was one which was hidden in blind Stephen's heart.

Much as he had thought of the Saviour, much as he had almost unconsciously learned to love Him, he had not fully understood how simple was the way to heaven until the evening, when, a little apart from the far-famed grotto and its crowds of worshippers, that unknown friend had told him what it was to believe on Christ, and "never thirst." From that moment, light had come into Stephen's mind, which had never been obscured again; and now he thought not wholly of a Christ once on earth to give help and blessing, but a Christ *in him, with him* always, sleeping or waking, at home or by the shore. It made him feel happy, strangely, sweetly happy. When he heard the children who went to some of the Sunday schools in the town sing snatches of a hymn which said—

> "Now I have found a friend,
>   Jesus is mine."

his face beamed with joy, for he felt it to be true—Jesus, the Good Shepherd, the gentle Saviour, *was* his friend, and would never leave him nor forsake him.

But the more he realised these things, the more in his childish way he leaned on Christ alone for salvation, so much the more did he feel dissatisfied with the religion of his home; and yet he did not know how to act as his conscience seemed to tell him.

However, Antoinette was not long in discovering that Stephen had always some excuse when she pressed him to go and receive the sacraments of the Church in which he had been baptized; and a few questions brought out the fact that he felt no longer any faith or love for those sacraments or that Church.

Stephen had expected his mother would be very angry, but to be aware of her bitter, hopeless sorrow, was worse.

With tears she bemoaned the time past, in which she had permitted him to be in the company of those whose words had "done all the harm," as she said; again and again she declared that God was sending another punishment upon her for her sins. So it was very hard for the boy, who loved his mother so deeply, who felt so grieved to be the cause of all the suffering she expressed.

One resolve Mrs. Le Breton quickly made—Père Guillaume must know nothing of this; she could not tell what might be the result for Stephen, and, strict Catholic though she was, her great, strong mother's love determined her to shield him.

"It breaks my heart, Stevie," she said, sorrowfully; "I would rather God had taken you from me when you were an innocent baby than that you lived to turn against the holy Church I love. But neither your father, your brothers and sisters, not even the Père Guillaume, must know of this. It is surely but a temptation, which will pass away; my prayers and penances must surely prevail at last. Only what to do now to screen you I cannot tell, unless, indeed—would you go to England, to the school for the blind, of which we have heard so much?"

"Ah, yes, indeed, mother," said Stephen. "Then they would teach me to read, and for myself I could learn more of God's Word. It is hard to go away from you, mother," he added, "but it is best so."

The matter was not difficult to arrange just then, for a lady who, some year or two before, had spoken on the subject to Mrs. Le Breton, was now visiting the island, and had renewed her offer to take Stephen back and place him there for twelve months.

The only hard thing was to account to her husband and the Père Guillaume for this sudden determination to let the boy go, when awhile before she had been so opposed to the very mention of it. "He would never get his sight now," said Mrs. Le Breton; "if Notre Dame de Lourdes failed to grant her prayers, she could hope no more, and therefore it was well for the child to learn what he could, and now so good an offer must be accepted."

When the question of his religion was brought forward, Antoinette, the strict Catholic, seemed strangely careless. We, who know the secret, do not wonder, but to Père Guillaume it was matter of intense surprise and of much displeasure that she could say that "Stephen had been well taught; he knew his faith certainly, and if he had to live amongst those who thought differently it was but for a year, and all would be well on his return."

So Père Guillaume might scold, Le Breton himself resist and expostulate, but Antoinette carried her point, and sent her boy away to England, though it almost broke her heart to see him go. And how she prayed for him to the Virgin Mother and many a saint, I could never tell you, nor need I tell that such prayers brought her no peace, no rest of heart.

And then, besides her distress on Stephen's account, there was a very uncomfortable consciousness that his simple faith made him happy, while hers did not do that for her; nay, she found herself saying almost unconsciously some verse she had heard him talk of, and even felt in it something very direct and soothing.

Poor mother! her heart was certainly away across the sea, with her first-born child, and eagerly she looked for news of him. When letters came saying he was well, and also that he seemed happy and was learning quickly all they could teach him, Antoinette Le Breton told the news proudly, for it proved she had done well in sending Stephen there; yet even such letters brought their own pain, for she marvelled that he *could* be happy away from his mother!

And did the boy forget her? Ah no! Day by day and often by night he thought of home, and all the dear ones there, and when his mind dwelt upon his mother tears would rise into his sightless eyes. Yet it was true that he was happy, for he was learning so much which away from that blind school he never could have known; and, best of all, he was beginning to read now from the Bible prepared especially for the blind, and, passing his hands over its raised letters, could find for himself some of the sweet words which he had heard long before from old Martha Vallère.

So without any great events the year went by; and Stephen Le Breton was taken home to his mother and his friends again, the same and yet so different.

Not only was it in knowledge that he had gained so much, but he had learned to understand more really what it is to serve God, to learn of Him "who is meek and lowly in heart."

Gladly he went back to the little cottage, and yet some anxious fear was in his mind, for how would it be concerning his religion? He could not any longer hide from his friends that he believed on Christ, and only Christ, that he needed neither priest nor sacrament to go to Him who is the "great High-priest;" but what would his mother, what would Père Guillaume say?

Little did Stephen imagine what was

coming upon the small village on the sea-shore—the trouble and desolation which would visit so many homes, and rob them of their best and dearest.

Hardly had he reached his mother's dwelling—before even one Sunday came to bring the difficulty of Mass-going to be surmounted, as God should show him how—a terrible sickness made its appearance, and the strongest seemed to fall victims the most easily.

And first of all this dread fever seized upon two of the Le Bretons' sturdy children. Marie and Henri in the morning had been playing on the shore, but by night they were tossing in delirium upon their little beds, and before the second night were coffined for a speedy burial. It spread to the town, and it was for the most part the aged and infirm who seemed to escape; even when there appeared to be a lull, the virulent fever broke out again and again. And it was such hot weather! Not a breeze to cool the tainted air, a sort of heavy vapour hung above the little island, and even the sea seemed lazy and asleep.

Before blind Stephen had been at home three weeks, he was the only one left of the Le Bretons' little family. It was strange that he had not taken the fever, for, as the children sickened one by one, he could not be won away from their side. Père Guillaume came to each one to administer the sacraments of his Church, but Stephen told them of the Good Shepherd who was waiting to "carry them in His arm," and thus he calmed them when they seemed afraid, and knew that they died happily because he had told them Jesus had come, and they were not alone.

But as autumn came, and the weather was cool, and the wind swept freely over the little island, the fever pestilence passed away, and Stephen was left to begin a quiet life with his sorrow-stricken parents.

It did not need eye-sight for the boy to know that his mother was weak and low in body, as well as troubled in mind, and he was more than ever docile and sweet to her.

It was very wonderful the many steps he contrived to spare her, how many services he was able to render in the household, and how, when the work was done and she sat down tearful and sad to think of her buried children, Stephen's quiet sympathy was her great and indeed her only comfort.

The neighbours wished to be kind, but there was scarce one of them that had not passed through the same trouble, and they were therefore as sad and downcast as poor Antoinette.

"Thank God, you've got one left!" said one woman who had lost all her children; and Mrs. Le Breton, pressing Stephen's hand tighter, was heartily thankful he had not been taken also, and yet she mourned for the rosy merry little ones who were gone.

"Don't fret," said old Mrs. Le Fevre, who had no friends or family to lose. "It's better far to see 'em die young than live to grow up to give you trouble."

It was true, but it was no comfort to the mother just then; her only real help seemed to spring from Stephen's hymns and Bible verses, for he sought to dispel some of her deep grief from the stories of Scripture he had learned.

As for Le Breton himself, his cheeks grew hollow about this time, his hair tinged with grey, and his stalwart frame began to look bent, though not with age. It was not alone the loss of his four younger children that troubled him—he knew now that Stephen had given up the Church in which he had been trained, and that instead of Mass, and fast, and penance, his trust was placed in Christ only. It was true he was but a child, and bound to submit to his father's will; and thus when Le Breton scolded and commanded, Stephen went with him to his church on Sunday. But he could not be persuaded to confess to Père Guillaume; and even when forced to Mass it was plain that he was praying after his own simpler method to God, and to none other. So the father was troubled about the boy, and there were even moments when in his own heart he felt it would have been well for them had Stephen died rather than live to go against the religion of his parents. But if he felt this, he never said so to Antoinette, who clung more than ever to her only living child—he *could* not when he saw how good was Stephen, and how obedient in all things but such as his conscience told him were not in harmony with the teaching of God's own Word.

## CHAPTER VIII.

THE winter opened drearily in Jersey that year; it came in with unusual mildness, the sky was of a dull leaden hue, there was little or no wind stirring, and the much-dreaded fever broke out once more. As for the church bells, they were ever tolling; and constantly there passed along the streets some funeral party bearing one they had loved to the last earthly resting-place.

Even those who were well seemed listless and languid, as if life was a burden almost too great to be borne.

The little village on the shore where the Le Bretons lived did not escape the general visitation of sickness, more homes were made desolate even than during the hot months of summer, and the watchers by beds of suffering prayed for the healthful breeze which seemed so long in coming, and which would clear the tainted atmosphere and save such as were still spared.

They were somewhat a neglected set of people in that part; no church had been built for them, as it was thought to be within a walk of the different places of worship in the town. A clergyman was rarely seen by the inmates of the cottages, unless, indeed, the cottages of Catholics, who received periodical visits from their priest.

It was at this time of sickness and trouble that a gentleman appeared in the island who was a stranger there, and who soon found his way to the cottages upon the sea-shore, especially those where illness was rife. What he was, those poor people did not ask, whether clergyman or minister, they never thought to find out; it was sufficient that he would come to any sick bed with the gospel message, that he would smooth the way to the valley of the shadow of death by telling of Christ, whose death brought life to sinful man—life for ever.

On Sundays, and sometimes on week nights, he would gather a little congregation together in the kitchen of old Mrs. Le Fevre's house, which he had hired for the purpose, and there tell them of the way of salvation, and read them passages from the Word of God, or set them singing the simple hymns they already knew.

Very deep and strong was the attachment of those people to Mr. Faulkner, who came to give them help and comfort in their sorest need. He came one day to call at the Le Bretons' cottage, for he had already heard much of blind Stephen; but Antoinette was cold and abrupt in manner, for she knew how angry would be her husband and the Père Guillaume if this stranger was seen there.

"We are Catholics, we have our priest to visit us," she said, stiffly, not asking the visitor inside her cottage.

"And your son, the blind boy of whom I have heard, is he a Catholic also?" asked Mr. Faulkner, gently.

Mrs. Le Breton was puzzled for the

moment. "All our children were born and baptized in the one true Church," she replied; "they are all dead but this one, our blind son; but they each received the last sacraments of the Church before they passed away."

"You have indeed had sorrow," said the visitor, looking kindly at Antoinette. "May I not come in and have a little talk with you? I should like to know your boy."

She could not well refuse this request, yet it was with somewhat an ungracious manner that Mrs. Le Breton led the way into the kitchen where Stephen was sitting, and placed a chair for this unwelcome guest.

But whatever were Mrs. Le Breton's feelings towards Mr. Faulkner, there was no mistaking Stephen's pleasure.

"Oh, sir, how kind, how very kind of you!" he exclaimed, with his face glowing as he heard who it was; "I know, sir, all about you. Old Mrs. Le Fevre told me how you are helping and comforting the people, and she told me too of your meetings, and how they love to come and listen to God's Word."

Mr. Faulkner did not make a long stay, but when he left he asked Stephen and his mother to come to the service on the next Sunday evening. "I will not ask you to promise me, but perhaps you will think of it, and see if it can be managed," he said, bidding both mother and son a kindly farewell.

When he was gone, Antoinette returned to Stephen. "This must not be, my boy," she said; "a fine trouble we shall get in with le bon père if this heretic preacher comes talking here; and your father too— I know not what he would say if he found him sitting in this kitchen."

"But he is so good and kind, mother," said Stephen. "Surely it cannot hurt us to listen to the words of a man who loves God."

"But he is a heretic, Stevie!" cried Antoinette. "We, as good Catholics, may not listen to him."

"Oh, mother, mother!" and Stephen's voice was very earnest. "Your heart tells you that I am no Catholic; you know that God has made clear to me the simple way by which we may alone be saved, through

Jesus Christ His Son, whom He sent into the world to save sinners."

Antoinette covered her ears with her hands, as if to shut out her boy's words. "Do not break my heart, child!" she cried. "I know your faith is shaken; I know that, through my carelessness, your innocent mind has been filled with poisonous doubts; I know too that some strange and terrible temptation of the evil one causes you to refuse to confess your sins to our good priest, as the Church commands. But oh, Stephen, it will pass, it *must* pass, and you will make me happy once more. For that I pray each day and night; and the Blessed Virgin, who knows a mother's heart, will hear a mother's prayer. I will not listen, I will not hear you say that you are no Catholic—else must I confess it to the Père Guillaume. No, no, Stephen, you are weak, you are tempted, you are sinning grievously, but Mary, the refuge of sinners, will gain you the grace of contrition at last."

It was the first time any such conversation had passed between Mrs. Le Breton and Stephen, and the boy felt deeply moved by her distress.

"Mother, dear, dear mother!" he said, and his voice trembled; "I love you dearly, more dearly than life, but I love God better. I cannot be a Catholic, I must keep to the Word of God, and do what that commands me."

"Oh! Mary, pray for him, pray for this unhappy child!" moaned Antoinette.

"Mother, dear, she cannot help you; she was the mother of Jesus, indeed, but still only a creature. It is to God you must pray, to 'Our Father in heaven,' mother, through His dear Son, our Saviour Jesus Christ."

Whatever Mrs. Le Breton would have said was stopped by the sound of footsteps they both knew well, no longer firm and strong and cheery, but slow and heavy, as of one cast down in spirit, as Le Breton really was. With illness, and death all sound them, he felt each day as if he might be robbed of wife and sole remaining child, nor was he satisfied about that child's salvation, for the priest assured him that should Stephen die remaining obstinate in refusing to confess, his soul must assuredly pass to eternal torments.

So Le Breton went to and from his daily work with a burdened spirit; and now as she heard him coming it brought tears to Antoinette's eyes, as she noted the change in his once blithe step, and the mournful tone in which he sang that which still remained his favourite hymn:

> "Mary, Mother, shield us through life,
>   Protect us from the ocean's strife,
>   Calm the wild sea, bid tempests cease,
>   Through thee we reach the shore in peace."

Ah, it was the strife and storm of life of which this poor earnest but mistaken man was thinking, its many sorrows, temptations and cares. It was not to Christ the great Comforter he looked for help, but to Mary, who though "blessed among women," was never meant to stand in the place of God, to pity, pardon, and help; it was not strange, therefore, that Le Breton's sorrow of mind was almost too great for him to bear, and that prayer brought him no peace or strength of heart.

For the first time during their wedded life Stephen and Antoinette Le Breton had one subject ever in their hearts, of which they never spoke to each other, and that was the change in Stephen. Perhaps both of them felt that to put their doubts and fears into words was to make it more certain that he was indeed a so-called "apostate" from the Church of Rome; perhaps both were still striving to believe that it was but a passing rebellion which had taken possession of their boy, and that Père Guillaume's efforts and their own prayers would make all right. Antoinette, also, had an uneasy consciousness of the fact that by the bed-side of her dying children, and in many a desolate hour afterwards, she also had felt a strange comfort in the Bible words which the blind boy had repeated, and in the sweet, simple hymns of which he had learned so many by heart. *Now* Antoinette was striving to shake off the influence Stephen's faith seemed to gain over her; but in the depth of her first grief she had taken comfort in it, and that remembrance was a weight upon her mind at the present time.

Thus it was that the Le Bretons said little or nothing to each other respecting the religious feelings of their child; whatever they felt was hidden in their own hearts, or told perhaps to the Père Guillaume.

As for him, he certainly spared neither time nor pains in striving to bring Stephen to a better state of mind, as he called it; but the boy had always some Scripture text to give as answer to the priest's arguments, and it seemed that no impression was to be made upon him. Had it not been that the Père Guillaume was of a gentle and kindly disposition, he would long before have pronounced the curse which the Church of Rome calls down upon all who are not with her; as it was, the priest still hoped that repentance on Stephen's part would spare such a blow to so earnest a Catholic as his father.

"Take courage, mon ami," he said, pressing the working man's rough hand kindly one day, when he had been pouring out the story of his grief; "hard as the boy's heart now seems, the power of God and the prayers of Mary can change it to a repentant heart. Pray much, mon ami, pray like the holy St. Monica, who was almost led to despair of the conversion of her son, yet who was encouraged when a holy bishop said to her, 'Go, and God bless thee! the son of such prayers shall not be lost.'"

"But, mon père, remember the sickness and the death which are all around us," urged the man. "Should it attack my boy, my blind Stephen, and his soul be called into the presence of God unrepentant, unprepared, what would be my agony!"

"I feel for you and your wife," said the priest—which he did truly. "We will pray that even if such is the will of God, mercy may be granted to the boy in that last hour. Many an one, who in life neglected God, has turned to Him at the approach of death, and, receiving the sacraments of the church, has been undoubtedly saved eternally; although much suffering in purgatory must be endured before the soul is fit for an abode in bliss."

That was all the comfort Père Guillaume had to give. As we have before said, he honestly believed all that he taught his people; and his church bade him believe and teach all that he had just said to Le

Breton. The father went home uncheered by such words, and his only relief was seeing day after day pass, leaving the blind boy unstricken by the terrible disease which raged around them.

## CHAPTER IX.

AT length, after many a prayer, after long and anxious waiting, the sun shone out once more, the atmosphere cleared, and once again the illness abated, and finally began to disappear from the usually healthy little island. It had been five-and-thirty years, so people said, since any contagious illness had raged there, and now it was hoped it might be many and many a year to come, before such sorrow and sickness should visit them again.

Stephen Le Breton, finding his wife and boy still spared to him, began to wear a brighter face; it seemed in part an answer to his prayer, and the rest, he hoped, would follow.

Though Mr. Faulkner was no longer busy among the sick and dying, he did not leave the village, as Père Guillaume and some others hoped he might, but, taking a house not far off, settled down among them to work for souls. It was not long before something of his history was known. From a youth he had but one great wish, and that was, to give his life wholly to God's service; but it had pleased Him who accepted the desire to withhold the health and strength which were needed to pass through the usual course of study for ordination.

During many an hour of weakness, many an hour of disappointed hope, George Faulkner had grown more and more sure that he could still work for God and for the souls of men, though not in the way his youthful fancy had mapped out; and thus he had begun to labour among the poor in his own native village, until such time as he saw more clearly the will of the Almighty regarding his future life.

There, he had formed the ties of a happy Christian home; there too had he buried his wife and child; and then it was that, hearing of the sickness and sorrow in the little Channel island, some strong impulse had led him there, to see if he could speak a word for God to those who were in sorrow. When this much of his story was known, the people felt more than ever drawn towards one who was so well able to sympathise with the bereaved and desolate; one who when he reminded them that "the Lord gave, and the Lord taketh away," spake from the depth of experience in his own heart, and not the mere utterance of the lips.

So Mr. Faulkner became a resident among the Jersey people, and only the Catholics looked angrily on him, and wished him far away from their island.

"Mind, he never enters my door again," Le Breton had said, when Antoinette told him of the gentleman's first visit; and Stephen, hearing this, had begged Mr. Faulkner one day when they met upon the shore, not to come.

"It only angers my father, sir," he said simply; "you see, he is a very strict Catholic, and he would get into great trouble if it was known that he allowed any one like you to come to our cottage."

"And your mother—is she also so strict a Catholic?" was the reply.

Stephen considered a moment. "I think sometimes she is not quite easy—sometimes she feels as if there was more help and comfort in God's Word than in all that Père Guillaume tells her; still, for all that, she is a Catholic."

"And how is it you do not feel the same as your parents?" said Mr. Faulkner; and for answer the boy told the story of his blindness, of the pilgrimage which had been made, of the Masses offered, of the prayers to the Virgin which had won no answer, and thus how the simple teaching of old Martha had come back to his mind, and he had begun to see that there was but One to whom prayer could be offered, only One who could grant help and pardon and peace.

It was the Sunday after that conversation that the boy resolved to go to Mr. Faulkner's meeting. His mother and father no longer forced him to go with them to their own church, though they lingered about and seemed so reluctant to leave him behind, that it was often a sore struggle to poor Stephen not to yield for the sake of pleasing them. But that he felt that he could not do so with a good conscience, he would certainly have gone; yet as long as he was not expressly commanded to attend, he felt that to join in worship which his heart had no part in would be a mockery; and, therefore, he had for some time remained quietly in the cottage or on the sea-shore, pondering over things he had heard from the Bible, and praying earnestly to God in his own simple fashion.

Often he had wished to go to the room where Mr. Faulkner preached, but reluctance to cause any additional sorrow to his parents had hindered him; on this particular Sunday he felt it would be a help and joy to him to join others in their prayers and praises, and therefore he went.

> "Let us with a gladsome mind
> Praise the Lord for He is kind;
> For His mercies shall endure,
> Ever faithful, ever sure"—

Pleasantly rang out the voice of the people gathered in the humble room; and after

Mr. Faulkner had read to them one of David's beautiful psalms of thanksgiving, and he had prayed to God in his own earnest, reverent words, as though speaking to One who, though great, was not far off, but a loving, tender, ever-present Father, he began his sermon. Scarcely a sermon, perhaps, but a plain, earnest address to his hearers in words which the youngest and most unlearned could understand; and as he spoke the men sat with folded arms and thoughtful faces, and the women with heads bent forward in eager attention.

He talked to them of the great love of God, he told them that all their lives long they had been like wayward children wandering away from the outstretched arms of a patient, loving Father, who wanted to welcome them back; and as he spoke many a sob was heard, and many a heart grew soft and repentant, and resolved from that time to leave the paths of sin and walk humbly in the fear of God.

Little Stephen came out with the rest, and strolled to his old seat on the rocks, with his heart full of happiness.

"Oh, how good of God to love us so!"

thus he spoke to himself; and there came the wish that it was possible for him to return a little of this great measure of love.

After a time the thoughtful look on his face brightened into a smile; and thus his father and mother found him when they came home.

"Why, Stevie, you look very merry," said his father.

"Oh, father, it makes me happy to know that God loves me so that He will take me to heaven. I shall have my sight there."

"Ah, heaven, indeed!" murmured the father, whose harder creed pointed him to suffering rather than to happiness after death; but Mrs. Le Breton pressed the boy's hand with a sudden painful fear.

"Don't talk so, Stevie! you don't want to leave me even for your bright heaven."

"No, oh no," he answered; "not till God calls me; and then, why, mother, I shall love to see the face of Jesus—I have seen no face on earth."

"Now come; father waits for his dinner," said Antoinette; and so they went in together, little thinking how soon blind

Stevie would be called home to the land where there shall be no darkness.

The next morning rose fair and bright, and Le Breton was stirring early, for he was going across to Guernsey by the steamer, about some business for his employer, not returning till the next night.

"Will you go with me, Stevie, boy?" he said half jokingly, and then added, "I have a mind to take him, 'Toinette; the change would do him good. Yes, my lad, you shall go, and I will get my business done, and we will be home to-night. We must not leave the mother quite alone."

Thus it was settled; and Le Breton started with his son, and Antoinette went down with them to the boat.

"Good-bye, my darling," she said, fondly; and then turning home she began to think how dear this blind child was, how good and obedient; perhaps, had God not thus afflicted him, he might have been wilful and headstrong, like so many boys—a trouble instead of her life's blessing; and in her heart perhaps for the first time she felt that the Almighty had been very merciful to her.

## CHAPTER X.

THE sun shone out, the sea was blue and calm, as Le Breton and his young son went upon their little trip, which was so soon over; and then they accomplished the business in the town of St. Peterport, and had an hour or two left for pleasure before returning home.

Being ordinarily busy with his daily work, Le Breton did not see much of Stephen, and had thought of him as a good quiet boy, with only one fault in his eyes, and that was his strange liking for what he termed a false religion. But now he found that the boy was thoughtful and intelligent beyond his years, and he began to consider what could be done with him by-and-by;

for it would be a pity that he should be useless as a man; and yet the blindness was a sore hindrance.

"I don't know what we are to make of you when you are a man, Stevie," he said half sadly; "you'll not do for a carpenter, and I can't think what there is for you; and yet 'tis a pity."

"I should like to help people to be good when I am a man, just as Mr. Faulkner does," said Stephen; "only I am afraid I never could."

The father's face darkened, but he did not scold the boy; this fancy for Mr. Faulkner and his religion would pass away, he told himself, and meantime the less said about it the better.

"I'll talk it over with the good Père Guillaume; he knows best," he said; and after a slight pause added, "if only you had got the right sort of music in you, my boy, you might learn to play the organ. I have heard tell of a blind organist. I can't rightly remember his name, but I suppose it was fine to hear him. Wouldn't you like to play the organ at the holy Mass or vespers, Stevie?"

"No, father, I never could," was the answer; and so the subject ended. Soon they had to go on board the boat, which touched there before going on its way to the larger island.

The evening grew chilly, for the sun had gone down behind a bank of threatening clouds, as they neared their home. The tides had been contrary during the passage from England, and the boat was behind its time.

"We shall never get into the harbour," said the captain; nor could they, and therefore the passengers had to come to shore in the small boats which always put out to help them in such a case.

Stephen, though seeing nothing, had enjoyed it all, for his father had described everything likely to interest him. And as he had sat still with the fresh air blowing on his cheeks, his mind was dwelling upon heaven, and its beauties, which he should see as he had never seen the beauties of earth.

"Now, Stevie, come on," said Le Breton, taking him in his arms carefully to protect him, as the people hurried to leave the steamer. "We shall get a bit of a tossing, my boy; but you won't mind that."

No, Stephen did not mind, for he was used to the sea; ever since his babyhood it had been like a friend to him, and he never thought of fear in connection with it.

"I can fancy the light in the cottage, father," he said; "I know almost as well as if I had not always been blind how it will look, and how mother will be spreading the table, and hurrying to get supper, and then coming to the door to watch for us."

"Ah, lad, I wish you could see your mother's face; but God's will be done!" said Le Breton with a sigh.

Whether the men who rowed were careless, or how it was no one could ever tell, but next minute they struck against one of the sharp rocks which make the coast of the little island so dangerous. The boat was upset, and those it contained were under the waves; but happily they were strong men, and able to swim, nor was the distance to land great. But Stephen! oh, I cannot tell you of the father's bitter grief, the mother's agony, as she wept over the lifeless body, which was washed up by the tide some hours later. He had reached the land of which he so often thought, and now had looked upon the face of Jesus his Redeemer. Happy Stephen! to have exchanged earth's darkness for heaven's light; but alas for parents, whose home was desolate and whose hearts were sad!

Yet there came a time when Le Breton and his wife felt that even in this great trouble God had dealt with them wisely and well. Not at first, but years after they learned the simple faith which had been given to their lost boy. Remembering his gentle goodness, the mother had begun to study his secret, and found that it was *love to Christ*. So, by degrees, she found her hope and happiness in believing in that infinite love, and by God's grace led her husband to cast himself for mercy at the feet of the "one Mediator between God and man," and look humbly and trustfully forward to the heavenly home He purchased with the price of His own precious blood—the home where Stephen was waiting to welcome them.

www.ingramcontent.com/pod-product-compliance
Lightning Source LLC
Chambersburg PA
CBHW020109170426
43199CB00009B/463